IMAGES OF ENGLAND

NOTTINGHAM PUBS

IMAGES OF ENGLAND

NOTTINGHAM PUBS

DOUGLAS WHITWORTH

Frontispiece: The Flying Horse Hotel viewed from the Exchange Arcade in 1949. Although now no longer a hotel, the mock-Tudor façade has been preserved.

First published in 2004 by Tempus Publishing

Reprinted in 2010 by
The History Press
The Mill, Brimscombe Port,
Stroud, Gloucestershire, GL5 2QG
www.thehistorypress.co.uk

Reprinted 2011

© Douglas Whitworth, 2011

The right of Douglas Whitworth to be identified as the Author of this work has been asserted in accordance with the Copyrights, Designs and Patents Act 1988.

All rights reserved. No part of this book may be reprinted or reproduced or utilised in any form or by any electronic, mechanical or other means, now known or hereafter invented, including photocopying and recording, or in any information storage or retrieval system, without the permission in writing from the Publishers.

British Library Cataloguing in Publication Data.
A catalogue record for this book is available from the British Library.

ISBN 978 0 7524 3243 4

Typesetting and origination by
Tempus Publishing.
Printed and bound in Great Britain by
Marston Book Services Limited, Didcot

Contents

	Introduction	7
one	Historic Inns	9
two	City Centre	21
three	The Meadows	41
four	Sneinton	55
five	St Ann's	67
six	North to Sherwood	77
seven	Hyson Green to Bulwell	89
eight	Radford and Lenton	109

The façade of Yates's Wine Lodge, Long Row West in 1978. This splendid Victorian drinking palace has been attracting customers for over a century – not only for its drinks but for its flamboyant architecture and intriguing collection of objets d'art.

Acknowledgements

My very special thanks are due to Richard Shelton whose photographs taken in the early 1970s form the basis of this book. He had the foresight to realise that the majority of the pubs of St Ann's, the Meadows and Radford were shortly to close and he began the task of photographing all the licensed premises of the city. I am also grateful to the following for the loan of photographs: David Archer, L.F. Brownlow, John Lock, Nottingham City Council: Local Studies Library, *Nottingham Post* and Martin Sentance.

I also wish to thank the following for their kind assistance: Geoff Blore, Dorothy Cross, Peter Golding, Elena Hayward, Derek Henshaw, Wendy Jels, Haydn Martin, Phil Meakin, Frank and John Northridge, Mark Sanns, Tony Shannon and Anne Trimming.

I am greatly indebted to Dorothy Ritchie and the staff of the Local Studies Library for their unfailing kindness and expertise and to my wife Margaret for her continued help and encouragement.

Introduction

The English public house is unique. Although replicas have been built in other countries around the world, none have the atmosphere of the real English pub. A public house may range in character from an old tavern, a Victorian street corner pub, a roadhouse, to a modern bar. All these have their regular drinkers as well as those who drift from one pub to another.

The building of public houses in Nottingham was at its height in the late nineteenth century. During this time new estates of houses were constructed in St Ann's, the Meadows, Lenton and Radford. Almost all the new streets possessed at least one pub or beer off-licence.

The naming of public houses tended to follow a brewery policy, either patriotic or mundane – names of royalty and the aristocracy were popular – or with less imagination, the pub would be named after the street in which it was situated. Following the tradition of an earlier age when an inn sign would picture an animal or bird, many public houses would still be named the Red Lion or the Raven.

Public houses built in the Victorian era were at their most opulent with ornate decorations, gas lighting, etched glass windows and glazed brickwork. The interiors of the pubs would be separated into distinct areas for different classes – a saloon bar, public bar and in some instances a parlour or ladies' bar, with a more plush decor. Fortunately, there are still a number of typical Victorian public houses in Nottingham which have not been spoilt by modernisation.

Nottingham also retains a handful of taverns from an earlier age, including the Bell Inn, Ye Olde Salutation and Ye Olde Trip to Jerusalem. The conflicting claims by these inns to be the oldest in Nottingham appear to have been resolved by Channel Four's *History Hunters* who decided that the Bell Inn had the most convincing evidence of its age, with records of ale having been served in 1638. The management of the Salutation took some comfort from the conclusion that theirs was the oldest building and the owners of the Trip claimed to have caves which were used as a brew-house to Nottingham Castle in the eleventh century.

Nottingham's city centre pubs, almost without exception, have caves beneath them which are ideal for storing beer at a constant cool temperature. This is one of the reasons why the caves were excavated in the first place – the earliest in the Middle Ages – and these have been added to over the years.

Nottingham has always been famous for its ales, achieved from the mineral properties of the local water and the barley grown in the Vale of Belvoir. Most inns until the middle of the nineteenth century brewed their own beer, a practice which gradually ceased with the founding of small cottage breweries, which supplied local inns and pubs. When the two major local breweries were founded – Shipstones in 1852 and Home Brewery in 1875 – most of the smaller breweries either closed down or were taken over by one of the bigger concerns.

Towards the end of the nineteenth century the major breweries began what became known as the tied house system in which licensees borrowed money from the brewery to purchase a public house. When the new estates of houses were built in Nottingham in the late nineteenth century, the Home Brewery and Shipstones vied with each other to obtain tied outlets for their beer. By 1901 there were 574 public houses in Nottingham; since then their number has declined to less than 250.

During the 1920s the Nottingham Corporation began the clearance of slum properties in Broad Marsh and Narrow Marsh. At that time, there were no fewer than twelve public houses in the district of which only the News House now remains.

With the building of new council house estates in the north and west of the city in the 1930s, new roadhouse style pubs were built on main roads. Many of these suburban pubs were built in mock-Tudor style, while others were neo-Georgian with the occasional Art Deco design. Traditional Victorian public houses had acquired a disreputable character and many were improved in order to attract a different clientele. Beer, which had been gradually weakened during the First World War was to remain at the same strength after the war when it was found that the public were happy to accept beer weaker than previously. At the same time, mild beer became the predominant drink with the more expensive bitter an occasional luxury.

The Nottingham pub scene changed dramatically in the late 1960s when the Corporation began the demolition of whole streets of buildings in St Ann's, the Meadows and Radford. Most of the houses were substandard but the public buildings were erased without proper consideration of their value. Of the fifty-seven public houses in St Ann's before 1965, only seven remained after the clearance of the area. A small number of new pubs were then built on the new estate, all of them without much character.

In the 1970s and increasingly in the 1980s food began to be provided in more establishments, although the standard of food could be, to say the least, indifferent.

Since the Second World War the drinking habits of the British public have changed considerably – keg beer and lager being the predominant drinks – doubtless because of the variable quality of traditional ale. However, in recent years, with the emergence of campaigners for cask-conditioned ales, an increasing number of pubs are providing two or three varieties of real ale.

The traditional pubs in the centre of Nottingham and the inner suburbs now aim to attract diners in greater numbers without making their regular drinkers feel unwelcome. An increasing number of pubs besides having piped music, provide live entertainment in the form of pop groups, jazz musicians and the inevitable quiz nights, karaoke and live football on widescreen television.

The centre of the city has in recent years seen the opening of a considerable number of new bars in vacant shops and warehouses, attracting huge numbers of young people, especially at weekends.

Nottingham still has a number of traditional pubs which have not lost all their character. It is still possible to do a pub crawl on Mansfield Road or Alfreton Road and sample good beer in a number of bars which have not been completely ruined by modernity.

The English pub has changed over the last century but it is essentially the same – a local where one meets friends and strangers to enjoy a chat and a drink.

Douglas Whitworth
June 2004

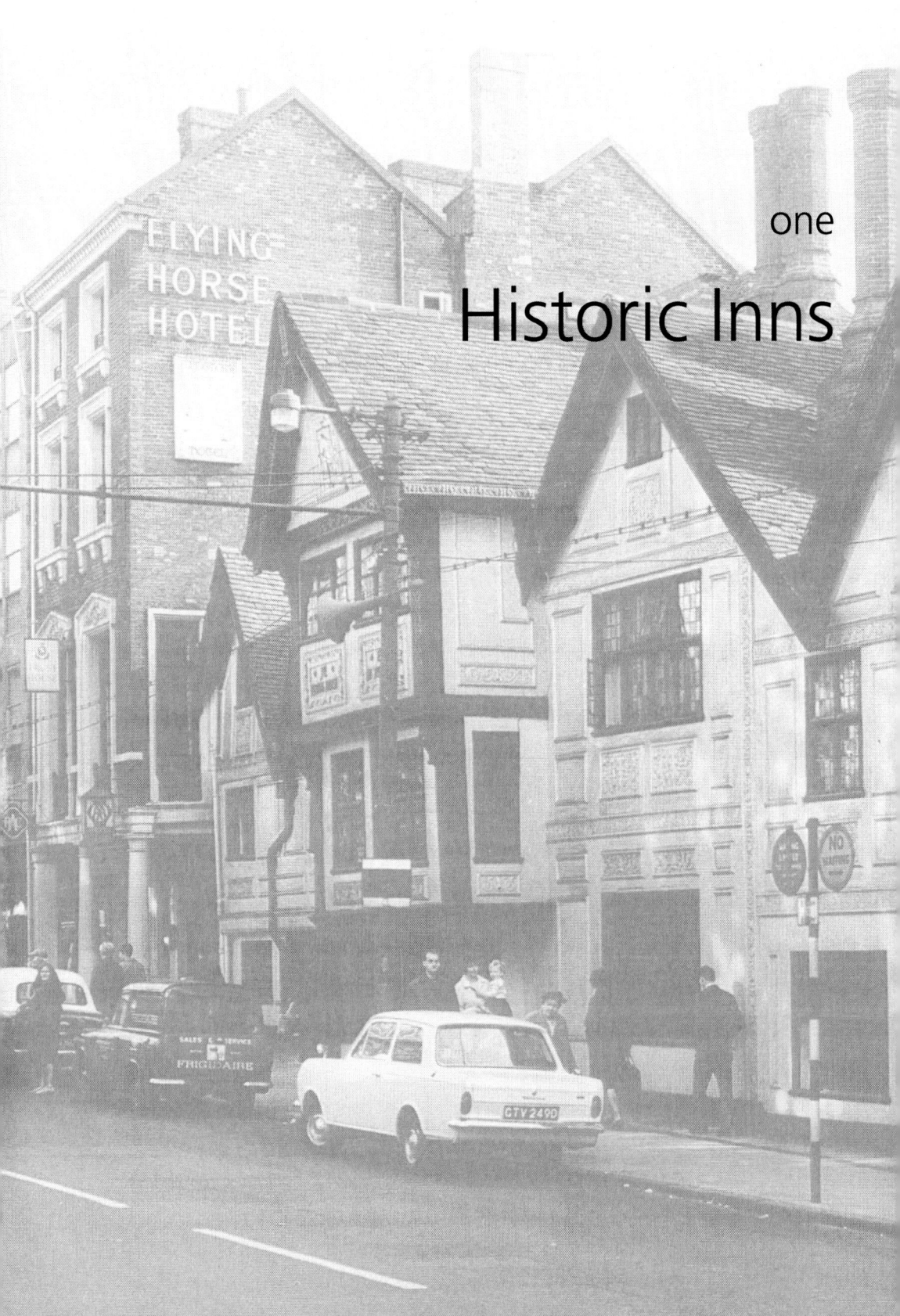

one
Historic Inns

The Coach and Horses, Upper Parliament Street, shortly before it was pulled down to be rebuilt in a similar style, *c.* 1903. This was a seventeenth-century inn, originally called the Waggon and Horses and later the Bell and Holland. The present pub has recently been refurbished, fortunately without losing its character, and is noted for its good ale.

Above: The Bell Inn, Angel Row in 1972. The Bell, now believed to be the oldest in Nottingham has monastic connections, for it was previously the refectory of the Carmelite Friary then sited on Beastmarket Hill. The original flagstones still exist in the main passageway down which horsemen and coachmen led their charges to the stables at the rear. In 1898 Joseph Jackson took over the Bell and for the next century the Jackson family ran the establishment, finally selling the inn to Hardy and Hansons in 2002.

Right: Ye Olde Salutation Inn, Hounds Gate, *c.* 1900. The history of the inn is far from clear – the earliest reference to the Salutation was in 1725 but the building dates from much earlier. The three levels of caves beneath the inn are certainly several hundred years older than the building, and were in all probability intended for habitation.

Above: Ye Olde Trip to Jerusalem, Brewhouse Yard, *c.* 1950. The age of this inn, the most famous in Nottingham, is conjectural. The first recorded evidence of the Trip was in 1760 but there is a suggestion that there was a brew-house named the Pilgrim on the site as early as 1611. Many of the rooms are caves cut out of the rock face and beneath the cellars is a cave that in earlier days was used as a cockpit.

Opposite: A re-enactment in 1989 of the legendary story of the Knights Templar halting at Ye Olde Trip to Jerusalem. King Richard the Lionheart with some of his Crusaders quaffing ale at the Trip - albeit in tumblers - as it might have been on the Third Crusade to the Holy Land in 1189. Clockwise from King Richard (Paul Parjer) are Ian Buxton, Neil Elverson, Dave James, Malcolm Perkins, Kevin Colgate and Robert and Craig Mawson.

The Royal Children, Castle Gate in 1924. The story of the children of Princess Anne, daughter of James II, lodging here in 1688 is unfortunately only a myth. The whalebone attached to the outside of the inn is, however, real and is now kept in a glass case inside the building. The inn was rebuilt in 1933-34, but has little in common with the old building.

The Gate Hangs Well, Brewhouse Yard in 1906 – the year in which it closed. The sign outside reads 'This gate hangs well, and hinders none, refresh and pay, and travel on'. The public house which was also known as the Hanging Gate, was one of several which once stood in Brewhouse Yard.

The Flying Horse Hotel, The Poultry in 1966. This famous inn bears the date 1483 on the front, which however, cannot be justified. The original building was owned by the Plumptre family who were founders of almshouses in Fisher Gate, but the present structure dates back to the seventeenth century. Records show that in the late eighteenth century the inn was known as the Travellers and later acquired the name the Flying Horse. The inn underwent considerable structural alteration in 1936 when its present Tudor façade was created. In 1987 permission was granted for the hotel to be converted into a shopping arcade with the retention of the decorative frontage.

Above: Yates's Wine Lodge, Long Row West in 1972. One of Nottingham's most famous haunts, this hostelry has a history extending over 400 years. Known originally as the Talbot, the Tudor inn was demolished in 1874 by Edward Cox who created the most ornate gin palace in the whole of the Midlands. The interior was filled with mirrors, brilliant cut glass, bronze statues, oil paintings and curios, making the Talbot an instant sensation. In 1929 Yates's Wine Lodges bought the Talbot and although many of the unusual items which filled the tavern have disappeared, Yates's is still a great attraction.

Right: A tower clock in Yates's Wine Lodge in 1965. This type of clock, built in the late nineteenth century by Cope Brothers, was more usually employed to drive external clocks on churches and public buildings. This clock, however, was used to drive a large dial which overlooked the main hall and also several smaller dials. It has a chime and strike facility and at one time had tubular bells.

Above: The Old Corner Pin, Clumber Street in 1972. This old inn began life as the George and by 1799 had become the Horse and Groom, before taking its later title in 1910. After its closure in 1989 the Old Corner Pin was converted into a Disney store and is now a branch of Miss Selfridge.

Left: The Lion Hotel, Clumber Street in 1989. The building dates back to the nineteenth century but its predecessor was a famous coaching inn named the Whyte Lion which fronted onto Long Row. The Lion's other dubious claim to fame was as a venue for cock fighting which took place in the caves beneath the cellars. Sadly, the public house closed in 2001 joining the nearby Crystal Palace and the Old Corner Pin where time has been called.

The Peach Tree, South Sherwood Street in 1972. Dating from 1761, the Peach Tree was a traditional pub until 1981 when it was refurbished and renamed Langtry's. The bar now displays posters and photographs of Lily Langtry who appeared at the nearby Theatre Royal in 1885. Next to the Peach Tree is the Turf Tavern, at that time these two were the only adjoining public houses in Nottingham.

The Old Angel, Stoney Street in 1972. The pub was established in the reign of Charles II and is one of the oldest in Nottingham. In the nineteenth century an upstairs room was converted into a chapel for the use of lace workers at the nearby factories and warehouses. Today the Old Angel is a typical inner-city pub with regular music gigs.

The Windmill Inn, at the corner of Pilcher Gate and Fletcher Gate in 1910. A Tudor inn, which was one of the least altered buildings from the seventeenth century still remaining in Nottingham in 1970. This was the year the City Council compulsorily purchased the inn for the purpose of road widening. Pilcher Gate is a reminder of the days when it was a street of makers of fur garments and Fletcher Gate is a memory of the flesh hewers or butchers who traded here.

The Loggerheads, Cliff Road in 1972 – one of the few old buildings still remaining in the Broad Marsh and Narrow Marsh areas. The pub, now unfortunately closed, dates from the middle of the eighteenth century and was previously known as the We Be Loggerheads Three. In the Victorian era, the thoroughfare was called Red Lion Street and was notorious for its overcrowding and crime.

Left: The Admiral Rodney, Wollaton Road in 1972. This was originally a farmhouse on the Wollaton Hall estate which, after receiving a licence to brew its own beer, became the Wollaton village inn. When Lord Middleton sold the estate to the City of Nottingham in 1924, the Home Brewery Company acquired the inn. In the past, the pub's outbuilding has had a varied use, being a schoolroom, meeting room and mortuary.

Below: The Ferry Inn, Wilford in 1926. This eighteenth-century inn, formerly a farmhouse, was at one time known as the Wilford Coffee House and later the Punch Bowl, but in 1860 it was renamed the Ferry House. The inn became popular as a resort for Nottingham folk, especially after the Wilford Toll Bridge over the River Trent was opened in 1870.

two
City Centre

The Albert Hotel, Derby Road in 1936, then owned by William Younger. The hotel was a favourite with commercial travellers and noted for its business lunches. Ladies were invited to the beautifully decorated coffee room after a lunch for 2/6d with no attendance charged. The Albert was demolished in 1970 when an inner ring road was planned for Nottingham.

The Hand and Heart, Derby Road in 1972. Named after a local Friendly Society in the 1860s, the public house has its back rooms built into the rock face. The pub's appearance has unfortunately been spoilt by the additional rooms built onto the front of the old building.

The Criterion, Angel Row in 1911, decorated with flags and coloured electric lights for the forthcoming Coronation of King George V. This short street besides having two public houses, also boasted three wine and spirit merchants; William Hickling,
T. Foster & Company and
I. Willatt & Sons. After the Second World War, Capocci's opened a snack bar here, but in the early 1960s the building was demolished.

The George and Dragon, Long Row West in 1972. Originally a seventeenth-century inn known as the Green Dragon it was rebuilt in 1879. During the last twenty years the pub has undergone several name changes, first becoming the Dragon, then in 1994 the City Gate Tavern before reverting to the Dragon. On the left of the public house is the West End Arcade which was built in 1927 to accommodate the butchers who moved from the Shambles behind the old Exchange building.

Left: The Fox Inn, Upper Parliament Street in 1972. Built in 1928 on the site of an earlier pub named the Fox and Owl, the building is surmounted by a fine stone figure of a fox. In 1989, although its street number is 67, the public house was for some unaccountable reason renamed Number Ten.

Below: The Tavern in the Town, Upper Parliament Street in 1972. It is now fashionable to alter a pub's name from its original title to a fanciful one, and this was an early example of such a change. The public house was originally called the Three Crowns, built in 1928 on the site of an earlier pub of the same name. The Tavern in the Town became Edward's Bar in 1997 before recently changing to Flares.

Right: The Parliament House, Upper Parliament Street in 1972. This is another example of a public house retaining the same name for over a century before being renamed — in this instance to the Princess in 1981. The latter title survived for only seven years, being replaced by Nico's, and shortly after that by the Cask and Bottle. The public house gave up the struggle in 2000 and is now a fast food outlet.

Below: The Turf Tavern, Upper Parliament Street in 1972. When Greenall's refurbished the pub in 1996 the house was renamed the Samuel Morley, whose statue stood nearby for many years until 1927. He was a prominent local philanthropist and was also a temperance campaigner. Infuriated regulars then launched a campaign to have the pub's old name reinstated. The outcry at the change of title had the desired effect and in 1999 the pub was renamed the Turf Tavern.

The County Hotel, Theatre Square in 1972, three years before its closure. Although not a public house, the County was one of Nottingham's notable watering holes, convenient for theatre and cinema-goers. The County began life as the Clarendon in 1869, changing its name to the Rufford in 1915, before becoming the County in 1923. When the City Council began the restoration of the adjoining Theatre Royal in the mid-1970s, the County Hotel was demolished to make way for modern dressing-rooms for the theatre.

Last drinks at the County Hotel, November 1975. Thomas Marriott, the manager, serving William Laycock with a final drink before the closure of the hotel.

The Wilberforce Tavern, Wollaton Street in 1972, shortly before its closure. In the foreground is Lomax's Hippodrome Snackery, where regulars came into town especially for his fish and chips. In the background is the Gaumont Cinema, which began life as the Royal Hippodrome – a variety theatre – and which closed in 1971. The Wilberforce Tavern has been replaced by the Royal Moathouse Hotel.

The Rose and Thistle, Wollaton Street in 1972, another old public house which has now gone. Beyond is the building which began life as Henry Barker's furniture repository and then became part of the Nottingham Co-operative Society's department store. All these buildings were demolished in 1977 to be replaced by a new extension to the Co-operative store.

The Blue Bell Inn, Upper Parliament Street in 1972. There has been a public house here since 1761, when it was known as the Bell. The present pub dates from 1904, being renamed the Blue Bell in 1928. The inn also has another entrance at the rear, in Forman Street, which was convenient for the printers and reporters of the *Nottingham Evening Post*, before the newspaper moved from the city centre.

The Spread Eagle, Goldsmith Street in 1972. This pub began life as the City Family and Commercial Hotel but became the Spread Eagle in 1952. Since then the public house has undergone several name changes, becoming Fagins in 1984, the Goldsmith Pitcher in 1994 – an allusion to the Goldsmith Picture House which was once to be found in the adjoining building – and now the pub is the Speak Easy.

The Robin Hood Tavern, Market Street in 1988. The building was originally the Alexandra Skating Rink which opened in 1875 but within a year it had become a variety theatre. For most of the twentieth century its role was that of a cinema, known mainly as the Scala but later under a succession of names. After its closure as a cinema in 1985 and its conversion into a tavern, part of the building became Loxley Hall. Here, 'medieval banquets' were partaken with re-enactments of hand-to-hand fighting between Robin Hood and the Sheriff of Nottingham. The tavern was shortly to close and after demolition an employment agency took its place.

A pair of Whitbread's magnificent dray-horses were part of a promotion for Dutch products in the Old Market Square in 1979. A young Dutch girl hands out drinks while a model sporting a Heineken tee-shirt poses on the back of one of the horses. A Dutch fairground organ was nearby as well as a bank of flowers.

Opposite above: The Imperial Hotel, St James's Street in 1972. The façade of the public house is Victorian, although the hanging lamps are reproduction. At the beginning of the twentieth century the building was considerably altered and in the 1960s further changes were made to the interior, and for some years the Imperial became a restaurant.

Opposite below: The News House, St James's Street in 1972. The pub has been in existence since the late eighteenth century and derives its title from the days when inns employed newspaper readers to impart the news to their illiterate patrons. For some unknown reason, the public house was renamed Bar Oz in 1997, but with the rapidity of name-changes nowadays it will possibly soon revert to its former name.

The Dog and Bear, Bridlesmith Gate, in 1972. The public house was built in 1876 on the site of an earlier inn of the same name, with the heads of a dog, a bear and their handlers on the front, and figures of the animals engraved on the window panes. After the closure of the Dog and Bear the building was divided between Starbucks Coffee House and Whittard's tea and coffee shop.

The Eight Bells, St Peter's Gate, shortly after it closed in 1960. The pub dated from the eighteenth century when it was also a recruiting centre for the militia. By the time of its closure the Eight Bells had a reputation for being one of the rowdiest pubs in Nottingham. Perhaps this was the reason why the pub was chosen for a scene in the film *Saturday Night and Sunday Morning*.

The Bodega, Pelham Street in 1972. The Bodega was built in 1902 on the site of the Durham Ox, a famous musical pub which by that time was rather dilapidated. The distinctive architecture of the Bodega remains with the two shields bearing its name still over the entrance, although there have been a number of changes of title in recent years. Initially, the pub was renamed Cairo's, and subsequently became Rosie O'Brien's, next it became the Pump House and is now the Social.

The Queen Elizabeth, Bottle Lane in 1972, a mock-Tudor pub built in 1928 on the site of an earlier inn of the same name. The construction of the Great Central Railway tunnel in the 1890s, which passed only a few feet beneath the Queen Elizabeth, gave the engineers many problems. The pub has now been demolished, to be replaced by a hotel and apartments

Warrow's Wine Bar, Fletcher Gate in 1972. One of the first wine bars in Nottingham, Warrow's had a continental atmosphere. The bar did not survive the decade, but with the revival of the Lace Market, the area now has many bars and clubs. The building has recently been demolished and the land has been redeveloped.

The Sawyers Arms, Lister Gate in 1972. The pub was built in the 1930s in Art Deco design, and stands on the site of an older establishment. During the Second World War it was much frequented by American and Canadian servicemen who, although allies, were often to be found fighting. In 1964, the pub became a Berni Inn with a Schooner Inn upstairs and a Victoriana bar on the ground floor. The Sawyers Arms closed in 1988 since when the building has become a retail outlet.

34

A reminder of the Pilgrim Fathers came to Nottingham in 1970 when a coach and four arrived at the Sawyers Arms, Lister Gate, carrying descendants of the *Mayflower*'s doctor. They were Margaret Rasell and her daughter Patricia, standing on the left – direct descendants of Captain Samuel Fuller who were taking part in a special journey arranged by Berni Inns, from Boston to Plymouth as part of the 350th anniversary celebration of the *Mayflower*'s historic voyage. The Lord Mayor of Nottingham, Alderman W.G.E. Dyer, Wendy George, (Miss Great Britain) and Diana Wray (Miss Boston) are also in the photograph.

BARLEY MOW
SHIPSTONES
18

SEVERNS
Beer Wines Spirits
SEVERN
MERCHANT
8
GOBLIN

Above: The County Tavern, High Pavement, with its mock-Tudor frontage in 1972. The pub was established in 1834 and was then known as the Cock and Hoop. In 1841 it was renamed the County Tavern due to its proximity to the Shire Hall, then an enclave of the county. When courts were still held at the Shire Hall, the pub was convenient for a 'quick half' for lawyers, clerks and reporters. The County Tavern was renamed the Cock and Hoop in 2001 and is now an up-market pub.

Opposite above: The Barley Mow, Weekday Cross in the early 1930s. Shipstone's home brewed beer is advertised, using a slogan borrowed from the Home Brewery Company. Vintage cars are neatly parked at the top of Middle Hill, now the site of the city's new tramline. The Barley Mow was pulled down in 1950 as part of a road-widening scheme.

Opposite below: Severns, Middle Pavement in 1964. James and John Severn began their wine and spirit business in 1736 in the Georgian house on the left. It was early in the twentieth century when the building on the right was purchased, but not until 1956 that a restaurant was established here. During the conversion of the building, the original medieval timbers were discovered beneath layers of plaster. However, the venture was not to last; when the Broad Marsh Shopping Centre was planned in the 1960s these buildings were scheduled for demolition. Fortunately, an alternative solution was found and the timber-framed building was taken apart and rebuilt on Castle Road.

Above: The George Hotel, George Street in 1972. The oldest hotel in Nottingham, it was originally a coaching inn dating from 1822, when it was known as the George the Fourth. Many famous people have stayed here including Charles Dickens and Henry Irving, and more recently Elizabeth Taylor and Richard Burton. The hotel is now named the Comfort – part of the Choice Group.

Left: Jalland's Vaults, Goose Gate in 1966, the year of its closure, when its licensee was W.A. Househam. This 155-year old pub was mainly frequented by the lace hands who either worked in the local warehouses or at home, clipping and mending lace. The vaults had the reputation of having the longest bar in England, above which was a famous two-faced clock. When the Lace Market's prosperity declined, Jalland's closed their vaults while retaining a wine shop. More recently the public house was re-opened as Browne's.

The Admiral Duncan in the left foreground of Lower Parliament Street in 1964. This Art Deco public house was built in 1935 when a new road was cut through the slums of Cur Lane. In 2000, the pub was given a new image as a gay bar with the name @ D2. On the far right is the Old Plough which has had a number of name changes, becoming Jacey's Bar in 1982, before being renamed the Ice Bar and is now a club with the enigmatic title OHM 47.

The Old Dog and Partridge, Lower Parliament Street in 1972. This pub, until 1970, was in competition with the Original Dog and Partridge situated across Parliament Street. The Original Dog and Partridge was the older of the two houses, but lost the battle when it was demolished during the construction of the Victoria Shopping Centre. The licensee of the Old Dog and Partridge in the 1970s was Jack Dale.

The Victoria Hotel, Milton Street in 1972. Originally known as the Victoria Station Hotel, it is now overwhelmed by the Victoria Shopping Centre and flats. The hotel was recently refurbished and has lost its old-fashioned image and name, now being called the Nottingham Hilton.

three
The Meadows

The Black's Head, Broad Marsh in 1931. Built approximately in 1900 on the site of a seventeenth-century house which later became an inn, this pub was shortly to be demolished. By this time, the whole area, along with Narrow Marsh, was already condemned as the worst slum in Nottingham.

The Town Arms, Plumptre Square in 1972. This Victorian public house, originally the Rugged Staff, was built at the bottom of Malin Hill, one of the ancient routes into Nottingham. When its licence was withdrawn in the early 1980s the pub remained empty for several years until in 1987 it was set alight by vandals and destroyed. During the subsequent demolition, many interesting caves were discovered beneath the building.

The Stag and Pheasant, Lower Parliament Street in 1987. A mock-Tudor pub, the Stag and Pheasant replaced one of the same name in nearby Poplar Street, which was demolished in the slum clearance of the 1930s. The new Stag and Pheasant was pulled down in 2000, as part of the redevelopment of the Boots Island Street site.

The General Gordon, London Road in 1972. This was one of the pubs that fans would drop into on their way to the city's football grounds. After a century as the General Gordon, the pub was renamed Old Tracks in 1992. The change was short-lived as the pub closed in 1995 and the building was converted into ten furnished flats for the charity Family First. A new road layout at this point in 2000 brought about the demolition of the building.

The Grand Central, Great Northern Close in 1987. This was originally the booking hall of the High-Level Station of the Great Northern Railway. After the closure of the line in 1967 the booking hall remained empty until it was converted into a restaurant and bar. For several years a shunting locomotive stood outside the establishment, which has now been demolished. In the background are the warehouses built by Sir Jesse Boot in 1914 and demolished in 1996.

Opposite above: The Narrow Boat, Canal Street in 1988, a reminder of the heyday of the country's canals. The pub was in the last years of its life, closing down in 1996. The inn, originally called the Bowling Green has now been demolished, with the rest of these buildings, to be replaced by the *Nottingham Evening Post*'s new headquarters and a British Telecom office. In the background is a British Waterways warehouse awaiting conversion to a series of bars and cafés.

Opposite below: The Canal Tavern, Canal Street in 1996. This old pub, situated only a short distance from the Narrow Boat, has a sign over its door commemorating the opening of the Nottingham Canal in 1792. Other signs advertise traditional hand-pulled ales and pub food. The Canal Tavern was demolished in the clearance of the area before its redevelopment.

BRITISH WATERWAYS
ELITE PIZZA & KEBAB HOUSE

The CANAL TAVERN
Riding BITTER & MILD
OLD BAILY
& other fine Ales
The CANAL TAVERN
Traditional Ales
Traditional Cask Beers

The Grove Tavern, Queens Bridge Road in 1972. Rebuilt in 1937 in Art Deco style on the site of an earlier pub, this must surely hold the Nottingham record for the number of name changes. The pub was first renamed the Miami Bar, then in 1988 it was changed to Ziggy's Bar before reverting a month later to its original name of the Grove Tavern. In 1992 the public house was given the name Tom Hoskins, from the brewery that owned it, and more recently it has become the Vat and Fiddle.

The Castle Inn at the corner of Wilford Road and Waterway Street in 1972. Although a well-built public house, this suffered the same fate as the majority of pubs in the Meadows in the early 1970s, and was demolished. The landlady at that time was Nellie Guy.

The Locomotive Inn, Wilford Road in 1972. A typical corner pub, the Locomotive derived its name from its close proximity to a railway shunting yard, and was frequented by many of the railwaymen. In 1965 Samuel Meakin retired after fifty years' tenancy of the Locomotive. The pub was demolished in 1975.

The Clifton Grove Inn at the junction of Waterway Street East and Blackstone Street in 1972. The pub was named after the famous beauty spot near the River Trent which in the past was a popular attraction to Nottingham folk. The last licensee of the Clifton Grove before its demolition was Frederick Pope.

The Griffin at the corner of Waterway Street and Lammas Street in 1972. In the 1960s a rag-and-bone man and his wife would visit the pub most days of the week with second-hand clothes which they would spread out for sale on the floor of the vaults. The last landlord before the pub's demolition was Thomas Henry.

The Crescent Inn at the corner of Bruce Grove and Ryeland Crescent in 1972. An unprepossessing pub, the Crescent was one of twenty-two licensed houses which were demolished when the Meadows area was redeveloped in the 1970s.

The Poet's Corner, Kirke White Street East in 1972. The pub's name is an allusion to Henry Kirke White, the Nottingham poet, most famous for his collection of poems entitled *Clifton Grove*. Since the demolition of this building in 1975, a public house of the same name has been built in the nearby Bridgeway Centre.

The Cricketers Rest, Kirke White Street in 1972. A Corporation cricket ground was situated nearby in the nineteenth century, and the recreation ground which took its place became known as 'the cricket', hence the name of the pub. The building was demolished in 1974.

Above: The Rifleman, Kirke White Street in 1972. This Home Brewery pub was rebuilt after the Second World War, but suffered the same fate as most of the terrace houses in the Meadows. New housing was built in the area, but the atmosphere of close-knit communities, all with their own local, had gone.

Left: The Nag's Head at the corner of Willersley Street and Cromford Street in 1972. Originally called the Eagle Tavern, the public house was built in 1860-61 when the Meadows were beginning to be developed. Three main roads were built through the district, with side roads constructed on a grid system, but since the redevelopment of the area, the logical pattern of the streets has gone.

Right: The Miller's Arms, Agnes Street in 1972. This pub, whose licensee was Ernest Taylor, was still open at this time but the adjoining buildings were already boarded up and awaiting demolition.

Below: The Greyhound, London Road in 1972, one of a handful of pubs in the Meadows which survived the redevelopment of the area in the 1970s. The pub, built in 1857, became known for a time as DC's Bar, before being renamed the Globe – a memory of the cinema which once stood nearby. On the right is a glimpse of the Burton Almshouses that were soon to be demolished.

The Star Inn at the corner of Waterway Street and Arkwright Street in 1972. Arkwright Street was then the main artery of the Meadows and was lined with shops in which almost anything could be bought. The public houses, invariably the first buildings to be completed, were the last to be pulled down when the area was cleared.

The Meadow Inn, Arkwright Street in 1972. The pub was built in 1860 when the Meadows were being developed – previously the area was famous for the crocuses which bloomed here every spring. The Meadow is seen here in its last days of trading prior to being pulled down.

The Cremorne Hotel, Queens Drive in 1972. Rebuilt in 1917, the pub was named after the Derby winner of 1872 owned by Captain Henry Savile of Rufford Abbey. The land at the side of the Cremorne was the site of occasional fairs known as the Cremorne Wakes which added to the attractions of this riverside venue. Unfortunately, the pub is now closed, with the land to be used for a housing development.

Three Dunkirk veterans sampling Burton's best bitter at 1940 prices in 1990 when they commemorated the fiftieth anniversary of the evacuation from France. Edward Willis, Arthur Thompson and Ernest Oakland were aboard the *Tamar Belle* on the River Trent, one of the 'little ships' that ferried soldiers from the beaches of Dunkirk.

The Town Arms, Arkwright Street in 1972. This Victorian pub by the River Trent is very popular with the city's cricket and football supporters. In 1984 the public house was renamed the Bridges, but within a year, for some unaccountable reason it was changed to the Aviary. After a period as the Casa the pub has been refurbished and renamed the Riverside.

A bear tasting a new beer at the Town Arms in 1978. The 34-stone bear was with its trainer, Andy Robin, the British and Commonwealth Heavyweight Wrestling Champion, promoting Hofmeister Lager whose trademark is a dancing bear.

four

Sneinton

The Grapes, Platt Street in 1929. The pub, kept by John Bowers, was shortly to close before being demolished. The area known as Sneinton Bottoms was to be redeveloped with the wholesale vegetable market being built on part of the land. Workmen are digging up cobbles in the street, while most of the buildings are already boarded up. Residents of the district were moved to new council houses in Sneinton but they continued to frequent the remaining old pubs of the Bottoms.

The Old Black Lion, Coalpit Lane, in 1929, the year of its demolition. This was one of the many licensed premises in a crowded district – there were no less than six in this street. The posters on the pub walls mainly advertise newspapers and magazines. One ponders the future for Arsenal's £30,000 wonder team – they were to win the football championship four times in the next six years. St Ann's Rose Show was also advertised promising prizes totalling £250.

The Fox and Grapes, Southwell Road in the 1950s. In the late 1930s, with its special early morning licensing hours, this pub became the local for the workers at the recently opened wholesale produce market. The Fox and Grapes achieved notoriety in 1963 when George Wilson, the landlord, was found murdered on his doorstep – a crime that has never been solved. The pub has earned the colloquial name Pretty Windows because of its decorative panes and chintz curtains, and although it was renamed Peggers in 1986, the nickname is still used. The pub is closed at present with its future in doubt. The 1950s was still the era of trolley buses as can be seen from the maze of wires overhead.

Opposite above: The Old Cricket Players, Barker Gate in 1972. The public house was rebuilt in 1884 on the site of a much older inn and derived its name from a cricket field in Sneinton. The walls of the bars were covered with images of cricketers and also photographs of the Nottingham Panthers ice hockey players. The Old Cricket Players has now been demolished and a block of apartments has been built here.

Opposite below: The Sir Robert Peel, Manvers Street in 1972. At one time, Nottingham possessed a dozen pubs named after noble knights, of which only two remain – the Sir John Borlase Warren and the Sir Charles Napier. The Sir Robert Peel closed in 1995 and was demolished along with the adjoining Boots building.

58

THE OLD
CRICKET
PLAYERS
THREE STEAK BARS
AND
FOUR BARS
OPEN UNTIL MIDNIGHT

SHIPSTONE
SIR ROBERT PEEL
SHIPSTONE

Left: The Earl Howe, Carlton Road in 1972. A nineteenth-century pub which remains almost unchanged, though the Nottingham Co-operative Society's off-licence next door has gone. Older regulars still refer to the pub as Billy Murphin's – the name of a previous landlord.

Below: The Duke of Devonshire at the corner of Carlton Road and Handel Street in 1972. A 1930s public house, known locally as the Madhouse from a period in the nineteenth century when patients at the nearby General Lunatic Asylum were allowed to visit the original pub here. The Duke of Devonshire now bears a plaque outside relating the history of the asylum.

The Barley Mow, Clarence Street in 1972 – a year after its closure. On the boundary between St Ann's and Sneinton Elements, the Barley Mow suffered the fate of the majority of pubs in St Ann's and was pulled down. The licensee at its closure was Elsie Gilbert.

The Roebuck at the corner of Carlton Road and Storer Street in 1972. The Roebuck, like the nearby Barley Mow on the edge of the St Ann's clearance scheme was to suffer a similar fate and was demolished.

Left: The Crown Inn, Carlton Road in 1972. The Crown was then well-known for its weekly flower show. Held at midday on Sundays, local gardeners combined drinking with displaying and selling their garden produce. In 1983 the pub which is now closed changed its name to Smithy's, an allusion to the forge that was once at the rear of the building.

Below: William Baker, the publican of the Crown, Carlton Road, ringing a brass bell for time in 1965, a custom that has existed for generations. William Baker played football for Peterborough City (now Peterborough United) and like many other footballers of that period, became a pub landlord at the end of his playing career.

The Red Cow, Windmill Lane in 1972 was probably the last pub in Nottingham, until the arrival of micro-breweries, to brew its own beer. The pub has now closed to be replaced by a block of flats.

The Smith's Arms, Sneinton Road in 1972. Originally a beer house, the Smith's Arms was rebuilt in the 1930s after the old properties in the district were cleared. The pub, whose landlord was then Harold Brown, has now been renamed the Lamp – an allusion to the old-fashioned lamp hanging outside.

IND COOPE
THE FOX
IND COOPE
LENNON
BROS LTD

HOME
BENDIGO
BAR & SMOKE ROOM

The Lord Nelson, Thurgarton Street in the 1880s. Known locally as the White House, the inn was originally two cottages built in the seventeenth century. Initially called Hornbuckles, this coaching inn on the Southwell Road was later named after the victor of Trafalgar. The Lord Nelson is a Grade II listed building and apart from now having high hedges surrounding the beer garden, little has changed.

Opposite above: The Fox, Dale Street in 1972 when the licensee was Reginald Blyth. The building in the heart of old Sneinton is one of the oldest in the area, dating from 1760. After being closed for several years, the building is now occupied by a firm of solicitors.

Opposite below: The Bendigo, Thurgarton Street in 1993. Replacing the Old Wrestlers public house in 1957, this house was named after Bendigo, the locally famous nineteenth-century boxer. William Abednego Thompson as he was baptised, fought fourteen contests, one of which lasted ninety-nine rounds and was never defeated. After succumbing to drink, he was converted by a local evangelist and thereafter became a popular preacher. After unaccountably been renamed the Hermitage, the pub has now closed.

The Magpies, Daleside Road in 1972. Built in 1957 close to the Meadow Lane ground of the Notts County Football Club, the pub's name refers to the team's mascot. The public house has now closed, to be replaced by a supermarket.

Nottingham Panthers' player/coach Terry Gudziunas cracks open a bottle of coins in 1982, donated for Cancer Research by the staff and regulars of the Magpies. Paul De'ath, the landlord, is on the right watching with other Panthers, the result of two years' collecting.

five

St Ann's

The White Hart, Glasshouse Street in 1972. The pub was due to be renamed Boots the Pub in 1982, but following an injunction by the Boots Company to prevent this, the house was called Owd Boots instead. At the re-opening, patrons who brought in a pair of old boots were given a free pint! The pub reverted to its original name of the White Hart in 2003 and with it, a return to its old image.

The Forester's Arms, St Ann's Street in 1972, seemingly isolated and awaiting demolition. The pub, near Glasshouse Street, has however survived the clearance of St Ann's. The street was previously a well used thoroughfare from St Ann's to the city centre via the footbridge over the Victoria Railway Station. In the 1960s, the Forester's Arms became the first gay pub in Nottingham.

The Bath Inn, Handel Street in 1972. Built in 1930 in Art Deco style, this was one of the few public houses in Nottingham of this design. The licensee at the time of the photograph was Mike Martin. After a threat of redevelopment, the pub has now re-opened.

The Robin Hood Arms, Robin Hood Street in 1972 – the year of its demolition. This was one of only two public houses in Nottingham at that time named after the legendary outlaw.

69

The Sir Robert Clifton, Bath Street in 1972. This l930s public house was renamed Market Side in 1982 and later B and E's Tavern before reverting, appropriately, to the Market Side, this being the nearest pub to Sneinton Market.

The Central Tavern, Huntingdon Street in 1972. Built in the 1930s, the public house is on the edge of St Ann's but is now part of the city centre club and pub scene. In 1983, in an attempt to improve its image, the pub was renamed Gatsby's, but it has since reverted to the Central.

Opposite above: The Britannia Hotel, Beck Street in 1972, with the tower of the Salvation Army Citadel in the background. The hotel was opened in 1934 by the Home Brewery Company but in 1964 it became a Berni Inn. In 2000, the building was pulled down and replaced by an apartment block.

Opposite below: The Craven Arms, at the corner of Woodborough Road and Alfred Street Central in 1972 when the licensee was James Beardall. This was an old-fashioned pub, where at weekends there would be a sing-song accompanied by a pianist. The Craven Arms was one of the fifty public houses that were demolished before the redevelopment of St Ann's.

Whenever
the Green Cross code
Simply good taste
One way

CRAVEN
ARMS.

The Mechanic's Arms at the junction of Alfred Street North and Vicarage Street in 1972, one of the few Davenport houses in Nottingham. The public house was spared during the clearance of St Ann's, and now run by an Irish family, is a genuine Irish pub renamed the Pride of Erin but still known locally as the Mechanics.

The Victory Inn at the intersection of Alfred Street South and Lamartine Street, with its windows and doors boarded up, in 1972. This was a basic corner pub of St Ann's, homely and without pretensions. The replacement public houses on the new estate were functional, but had little character.

Left: The Criterion at the junction of Alfred Street South and Plantagenet Street in 1972 – one of the eight public houses in this street at that time – all now demolished. To the right of the photograph is a Pork Farms van parked outside the original premises of Frederick William Farnsworth, the pork butcher whose business grew to become Pork Farms, the well known pork pie manufacturer.

Below: The Alfred the Great public house on the corner of Alfred Street South and Roden Street in 1972. A well-built pub, typical of many Shipstone's corner properties with its main door at the road junction. The building was demolished in 1973 and the last licensee was Lynda Bates.

Left: The Zetland Arms, Welbeck Street in 1972. An unusual name for an English pub, Zetland being the alternative for Shetland, the most northerly islands in the British Isles. The pub was demolished in 1973.

Below: The Sycamore, Hungerhill Road in 1972. One of the new breed of pubs which were built in St Ann's in the 1970s, the Sycamore replaced the pub of the same name in Sycamore Street.

Above: The Napoleon at the corner of St Ann's Well Road and Northumberland Street in 1972, shortly before its demolition. The pub was popular with American servicemen who drank in the upstairs room during the Second World War.

Below: The General Havelock, St Ann's Well Road in 1972, with road works making difficulties for its regulars. The licence of the General Havelock was transferred to the Beacon, built in 1974 on Blue Bell Hill Road on the rise of the hill in the distance.

The Garden Gate, St Ann's Well Road in 1972, still open but standing alone in an area of demolition. The Garden Gate was replaced by the Chase in Chase Precinct in 1973.

The Lord Alcester at the corner of Pym Street and St Matthias Road in 1972 – one of the few public houses to survive the redevelopment of St Ann's. Relatively unknown now, Lord Alcester was a famous naval commander when this pub was built in the 1880s.

six

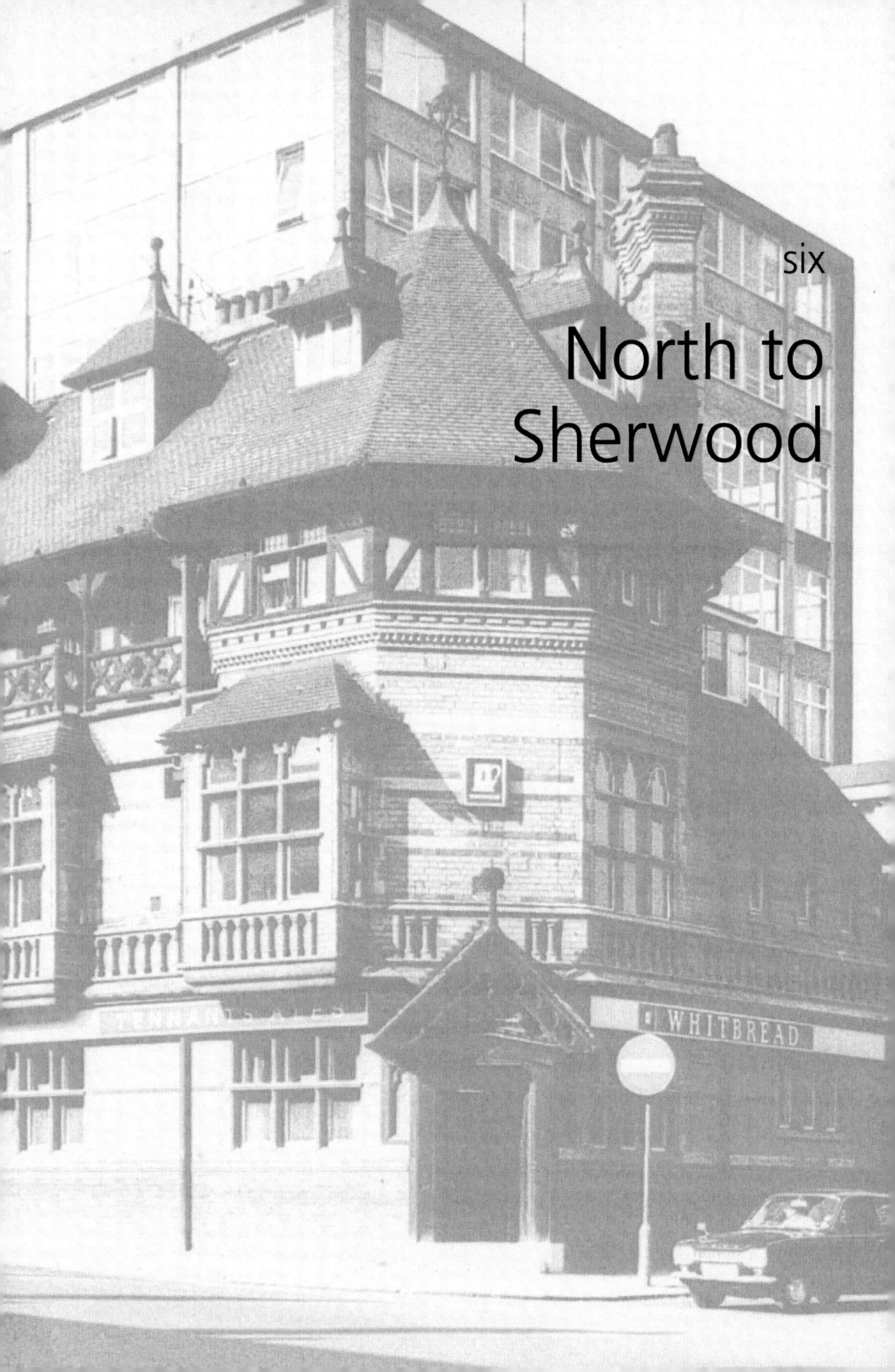

North to Sherwood

Left: The Mansfield Arms, Mansfield Road in 1972. This pub dates back to 1894 and retained the name of Mansfield Arms for the first eighty years of its existence. Since 1973 there has been a succession of changes in its title. It first became the Regent, then in 1983 it was renamed Blueberries, before changing to Ledgers in 1988. It is now called Bensons.

Below: The Peacock, Mansfield Road in 1972. This pub was rebuilt in 1884 on the site of an older inn of the same name. The Peacock has always been an unassuming pub, and still gives table service at the ringing of a handy bell.

Opposite above: The Roebuck, Mansfield Road in 1972. After almost a century without change, it underwent a succession of name changes. In 1981 the pub became known as Old Moore's Tavern. Its name then changed to the Empire in 1985 and lastly to Bobby Brown's Café before it gave up the struggle in 1995 when it closed down.

Opposite below: The Yorker, Mansfield Road in 1972. This famous and architecturally striking public house had recently acquired the first of a number of its name changes when this image was taken. The hotel was built in 1898 by Watson Fothergill with the title of the Rose of England which it inherited from a recently demolished pub. For a brief spell the Yorker became the City Alehouse before changing to the Filly and Firkin and in 2000 reverting to the Rose of England.

BROOKPARK
SURANCE BROKERS
LIMITED
WHITBREAD
WHITBREAD

WHITBREAD

The Nag's Head, Mansfield Road in 1944 – an old coaching inn dating back to the fifteenth century. In the days when public hangings took place near the present day St Andrew's church, the execution procession paused here for the condemned prisoner to have a final drink. The Nag's Head has recently been renovated with the loss of much of its character.

Opposite above: The Old Grey Nag's Head, Mansfield Road in 1972. The pub began life in the 1830s as a beer house, but became the Old Grey Nag's Head later in the nineteenth century to distinguish it from the Nag's Head opposite. In 1989, after taking over the adjoining premises, the pub was renamed the Lincolnshire Poacher and has now established itself as one of Nottingham's top real ale houses.

Opposite below: The Forest Tavern, Mansfield Road in 1972. Another old-fashioned tavern which sells real ale on the Mansfield Road pub run. For late night drinkers, the Maze at the rear is licensed until 2 a.m.

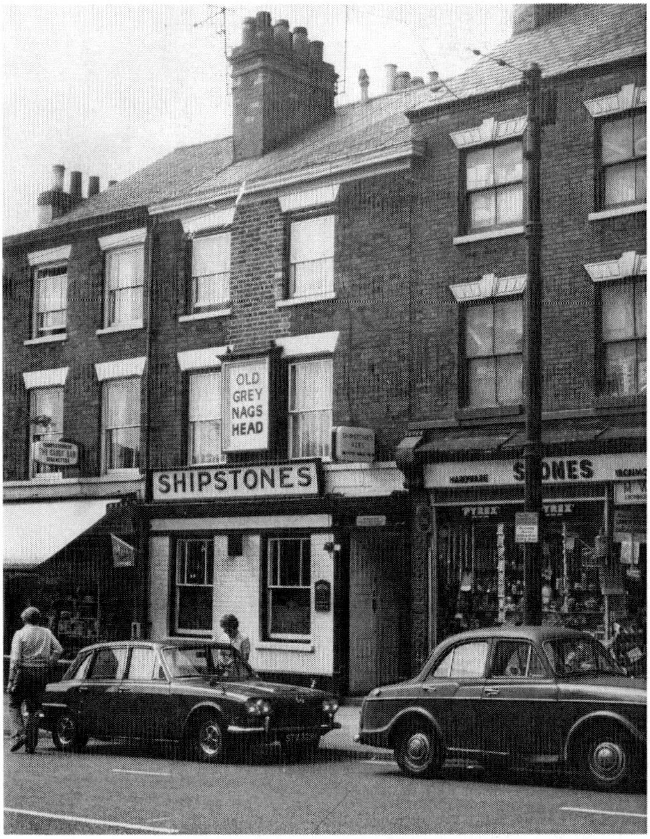
OLD
GREY
NAGS
HEAD
SHIPSTONES
PYREX

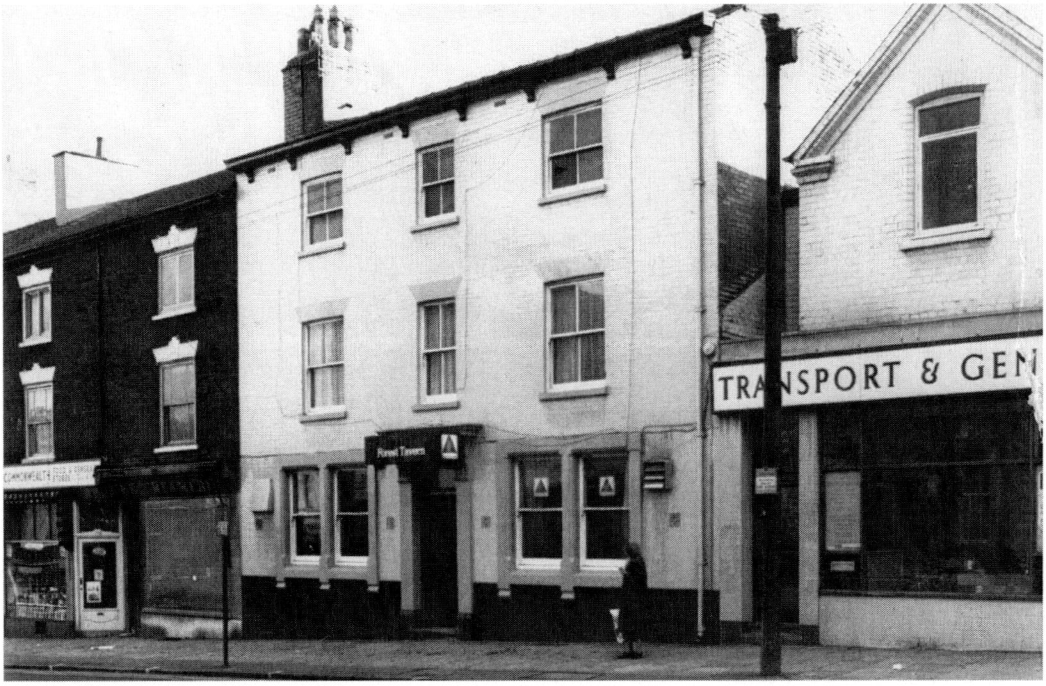
TRANSPORT & GEN

Left: The Duke of St Albans, North Sherwood Street in 1972. Claiming to be the smallest pub in Nottingham, these premises opened in 1927 and closed in 1963 when the building became a private dwelling.

Below: The Clinton Arms, Shakespeare Street in 1972. A change of name in 1983 to Russells, heralded a rather unsavoury period with topless barmaids serving drinks, which was fortunately short-lived. The premises are now named the Orange Tree and have become very popular with students from the nearby Nottingham Trent University.

The Newcastle Arms, North Sherwood Street in 1972. Originally the Duke of Newcastle's Arms, the pub was created from three houses. In common with many public houses, the interior was opened up into one large room. The pub has now unfortunately closed.

Ye Hole in Ye Wall, North Sherwood Street in 1972. Rebuilt in the 1930s, this pub has a series of caves underground which once linked it to neighbouring buildings. The pub underwent major refurbishment in 1984 and now serves traditional cask beers.

The Sir Charles Napier, Sherwood Street North in 1972. The pub is named after the officer in command of the troops who suppressed the Chartist riots on the Forest in 1839. The interior of the pub is little changed, with a door behind the bar leading to two levels of caves beneath the building.

The Saracen's Head, North Sherwood Street in 1972. From being an old-fashioned pub, the Saracen's Head now serves cask-conditioned real ale. The outside wall of the pub now has a colourful depiction of a Saracen brandishing a scimitar.

The Vernon Arms, Waverley Street in 1972. The pub stands on the site of a coffee-house and bowling green which was a well known rendezvous in the seventeenth and eighteenth centuries. Waverley Street was then known as Bowling Alley Lane. With Nottingham's new trams passing its door, the Vernon Arms will no doubt attract more customers for its real ales.

The Grosvenor, Mansfield Road in 1972 when it was a Berni Inn. The Grosvenor was built on the site of an earlier beer house called the Black's Head and derives its name from the horse which won the last race held in 1890 at the nearby Forest racecourse. The statue of the horse above the gatehouse has now been removed following vandalism.

Above: The New Inn at the corner of Mansfield Road and New Street in 1972. The pub has changed little over the years apart from its name which has now become Rosie O'Briens.

Left: The Gladstone, Loscoe Road in 1972. An old-fashioned pub which now serves several brews of real ale. There are regular concerts held here and the pub also has a large library of books.

The Sherwood Inn, Mansfield Road, *c.* 1890. The pub was already fifty years old when this photograph, with its widely spaced subjects, was taken. The brewhouse which preceded the New Inn was known as Widow Palethorpe's from the name of the owner. During the nineteenth century, the inn was a post-house on the edge of Sherwood Forest, with stabling for horses. In 1898 a ground floor extension was added to the front of the building.

The Robin Hood Hotel, Mansfield Road in 1972. An old-established public house and now the only one in Nottingham bearing the famous local outlaw's name. An inn has stood here since 1830, but the present building is a 1920s structure.

The Fox Hotel, Valley Road in 1972, when the licensee was Eric Read. The pub was one of the roadhouses that were constructed in the 1930s on the city's new housing estates. They were built to be impressive, with numerous facilities, including a lounge bar, public bar, function room and children's play area.

seven

Hyson Green to Bulwell

Left: The Smith's Arms, at the corner of Radford Road and Hyson Street in 1972, with a sign on the side of the building advertising John Robinson's noted ales. The public house has now been converted into a shop.

Below: The Radford Arms, Radford Road in 1972. The pub, originally the New Inn, was constructed within a month in the 1880s by a builder named Morrison to win a wager of £100. The pub has suffered the fate of many other inner city licenced houses and has now closed.

Right: The Albany Hotel, Birkin Avenue in 1972. The Albany was rebuilt in 1881 and is one of the few pubs in Nottingham to be licensed for music hall entertainments. Among the artists to have appeared here are George Formby and Vesta Tilley and a variety performance was broadcast from the public house in 1936.

Below: Keith and Dierdre Whittam, the licensees of the Newcastle Arms, Nuthall Road raising their tankards in 1983. The couple were celebrating becoming finalists in the *Nottingham Evening Post* Buchanan Booth's 'Mine Host' contest.

The Wheatsheaf Inn, Bobbers Mill Crossing in 1930 when the landlord was Robert Chadwick. The pub was shortly to be demolished, and at the same time the nearby railway level crossing closed and a bridge was then built over the LMS line. An ice-cream vendor has a prime position for passing trade, young and old.

The Wheatsheaf, Nuthall Road in 1972. The pub was built on Bonser's Field in 1931, near to the original pub, pictured above. This imposing hostelry was intended not only for local residents, but also for passing trade. Instead of bicycles leaning against the railings of the pub, sleek motorcars now park outside the premises.

Left: The Avenue Hotel, Birkin Avenue in 1972. A Victorian commercial pub, originally named the Birkin Avenue Tavern but always known locally as the Clock due to the public clock on the corner of the building. In 1986 the brewery and the regulars were of one mind when the pub was officially renamed the Clock. Although the surrounding area has been redeveloped, the pub remains, with the strange title, the Wheel Tappers at the Clock.

Below: Regulars and staff drink to the reprieve of the Lion, Mosley Street, in 1976. This typical back street pub was threatened with demolition but at the last minute was saved and still survives. The city's new trams stop only yards from the Lion which has been included in the *Beer by Tram Guide* produced by CAMRA.

The Old General, Radford Road in 1960. A pub, perhaps more famous for the historical character after which it is named, than for itself. The Old General was Benjamin Mayo, a simpleton who was a self-styled general of street urchins in the early nineteenth century. A stone statue of the general was erected outside the pub in 1878, but the present figure above the doorway is a plaster cast of the original.

Benjamin Mayo, the Old General. Ben was a familiar figure in Nottingham in the nineteenth century, especially so on Micklethorn Mondays, when twice a year the Micklethorn Jury would beat the bounds of the Borough. Benjamin Mayo would then gather a raggle taggle troop of boys to march with the Jury to ensure the school children were aware of the boundaries of the parishes.

An old-time music hall evening at the Elm Tree, Beech Avenue in 1975. Several of the regulars are giving a rendition of Down at the old Bull and Bush in the type of clothes their grandparents may have worn. Lined up on the piano are some of the prizes for the best and most innovative costumes. The Elm Tree has had its last old-time evening, joining the list of lost pubs.

A pair of Shipstone's greys on Radford Road in 1968. These splendid shire horses pulling a dray loaded with barrels of beer were then still a common sight on the city's roads. Shipstone's Star Brewery retained their stable of horses for publicity purposes for some years after they stopped being considered essential. The brewery finally closed in 1994 and the buildings have been converted into an auction house, offices and apartments.

Left: The Scotholme Hotel, Radford Road in 1972. Although recently refurbished, the pub has now closed.

Below: The Rose and Crown at the corner of North Gate and Monsall Street in 1972 when the landlord was Harvey Mather. A well-built house, the pub was demolished in 1987 to be replaced by Viva Imaging Ltd.

The Star Inn at the busy junction of Nottingham Road and North Gate in 1972 when the licensee was C.R.L. Baxter. This area of Nottingham has suffered from piecemeal demolition though this pub has luckily survived.

The Clinton Arms, at the junction of Radford Road and Eland Street in 1972. The pub which was famous for its Terminus Bar which displayed prints of public transport from an earlier age is now closed.

Above: The Shoulder of Mutton, Radford Road. From having a traditional pub name, this house first changed to the equally acceptable Windmill and then in 1985 to the absurd Thingamajigs and Wotsits. Fortunately this title only survived for four years before the public house was renamed the Rocket. The pub, however, was not to survive, closing in 1992 to become a McDonald's diner.

Right: The Fox and Crown, Church Street in 1972. The pub has a history stretching back to 1707 when it was both an inn and a debtor's prison. The premises were known locally as the Bowling Green from the rink which existed at the rear of the premises. The Fox and Crown is now noted for its fine ales which are brewed in the pub's own micro brewery which can be seen in operation from a specially built viewing gallery.

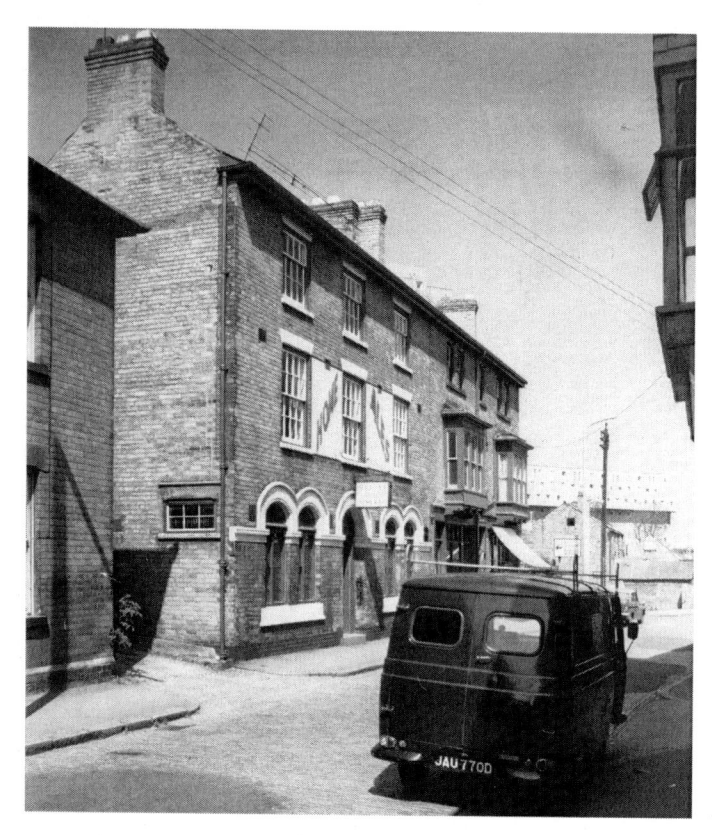

Left: The Mason's Arms, Church Street in 1972. The pub was replaced in 1992 by a housing complex named the Prince of Wales Court.

Below: The Duke of Newcastle, Whitemoor Road in 1972. The pub which stands prominently at the top of Bailey Street has recently closed to be converted into flats.

Above: The Old English Gentleman, Brown's Croft, shortly before its demolition in 1964. The young girls are posing for a photograph at the gate to the pub yard, while the boy on the right mimics David Bailey.
All the buildings in this area of Old Basford were shortly to be pulled down before the construction of multi-storey blocks of flats. These flats were to remain for less than fifteen years due to their poor construction.

Left: The Old Pear Tree, Bulwell Lane in 1972. Beginning life as a seventeenth-century farmhouse, it then became a beer house and staging post. One of the Old Pear Tree's tiny rooms is full of aircraft memorabilia from the time when it was the headquarters of a local enthusiasts' club. Another pub which suffered from the smoking ban and finally closed.

The Cocked Hat, Broxtowe Lane in 1972. This mock-Tudor pub was opened in 1933 on the newly built Broxtowe council house estate. The pub's signboard is unusual as it has a General on one side and an Admiral on the other – both wearing tricorn hats. The pub has now been demolished.

An American serviceman of the 508th Infantry Parachute Regiment, in the centre with a cigar, and locals at the Cocked Hat in 1944. The serviceman had just returned from duty in France having landed in Normandy on D-Day and been in continuous action for thirty-one days.

Teddy boys shaking, rattling and rolling with or without a partner at the Cocked Hat in 1956. The youths are in long drape jackets, drainpipe trousers and crepe soled shoes, and all have Brylcreemed hair with a huge quiff. For girls, circular skirts were all the rage and their hair was styled in a pony-tail.

Left: The Catchem's Corner, Vernon Road in 1972. The junction of Vernon Road and Bulwell Lane took its name from the owner of a shop situated at this corner before the pub was built in 1878. The public house was originally named the Station Hotel, but in 1969 it acquired its later and popular name. The pub is now closed.

Below: The Highbury Vale, Highbury Road in 1972. The pub has recently closed and been converted into flats.

Right: The Bull and Butcher, Main Street in 1972 – one of nine public houses on this street at the time. In 1986 this house was renamed the Bull, but shortly afterwards it received the unconventional title, the Tut 'n' Shive. The pub was pulled down when Bulwell Market Place became partly pedestrianised.

Below: The Horse and Jockey, Main Street in 1972. The pub was a prominent landmark in Bulwell Market Place until it was pulled down in 1996 to be replaced by retail outlets.

Left: The Horseshoe Inn, Station Road in 1972. This has been a pub for over 150 years and at one time had a blacksmith's forge at the rear. The Horseshoe was also used for storing coffins when the adjoining funeral parlour became short of space. Another macabre association was the hanging post which stood outside the inn in the nineteenth century.

Below: The Framesmith's Arms, Main Street in 1972. Known locally as the Monkeys from an earlier landlord's pet animal. The pub bears a sign of a monkey swinging in a tree.

The Mason's Arms, Commercial Road in 1972. Known to its regulars as Mad Jack's, the pub has the Masonic sign on the front. The public house was pulled down when the area was redeveloped.

The Cooper's Arms, Commercial Road in 1972. One of the oldest pubs in Bulwell, the Cooper's Arms was originally named the Lime Kiln and later the Top House but is now closed.

The Red Lion, Coventry Road in 1972. Bearing one of the commonest pub names, the Red Lion was shortly to close to be converted into a community centre. The wasteland in the foreground has also been adapted for community use as a children's playground.

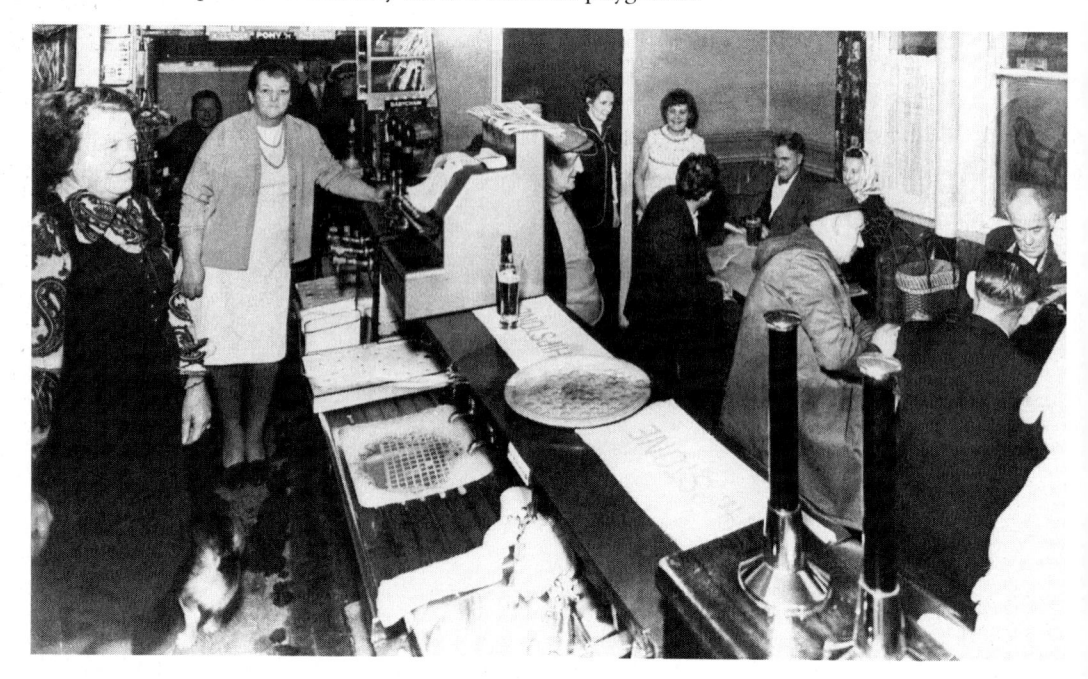

The last night at the Red Lion, Coventry Road in 1972. The regulars appear cheerful even though their local was about to close down, perhaps realising it was only a short distance to the many other pubs on Bulwell's Main Street.

eight
Radford and Lenton

The Marquis of Waterford, Ortzen Street in 1972 when the licensee was James Ormond. All these buildings were soon to be demolished in the wholesale clearance of the area.

The Albion, at the corner of Gamble Street and Newdigate Street in 1972. Although the Albion was a well built pub, it was pulled down in the redevelopment of the district.

Above: The Larkdale Inn, Oliver Street in 1972. A pub created from two houses, the Larkdale was another property shortly to be demolished and replaced by a residential building.

Right: The Sir Walter Raleigh, Raleigh Street in 1972. Although several other pubs in the area have disappeared, this fine old inn has fortunately survived and after a period as O'Rourke's has been renamed the Sir Walter Raleigh. This is the street from which the famous bicycle company took its name. It was in 1887 when Henry Bowden took over a Raleigh Street concern and created the world's largest cycle manufacturing company.

Left: The Queen Hotel, Alfreton Road in 1972. The pub is now the Queen Mary's and boasts a fine portrait of the Tudor Queen on the corner of the building.

Below: Regulars playing darts in the Queen Hotel, Alfreton Road in 1978. A form of darts was played in the Middle Ages when it was a training game for English archers; it became popular in pubs and taverns in the nineteenth century.

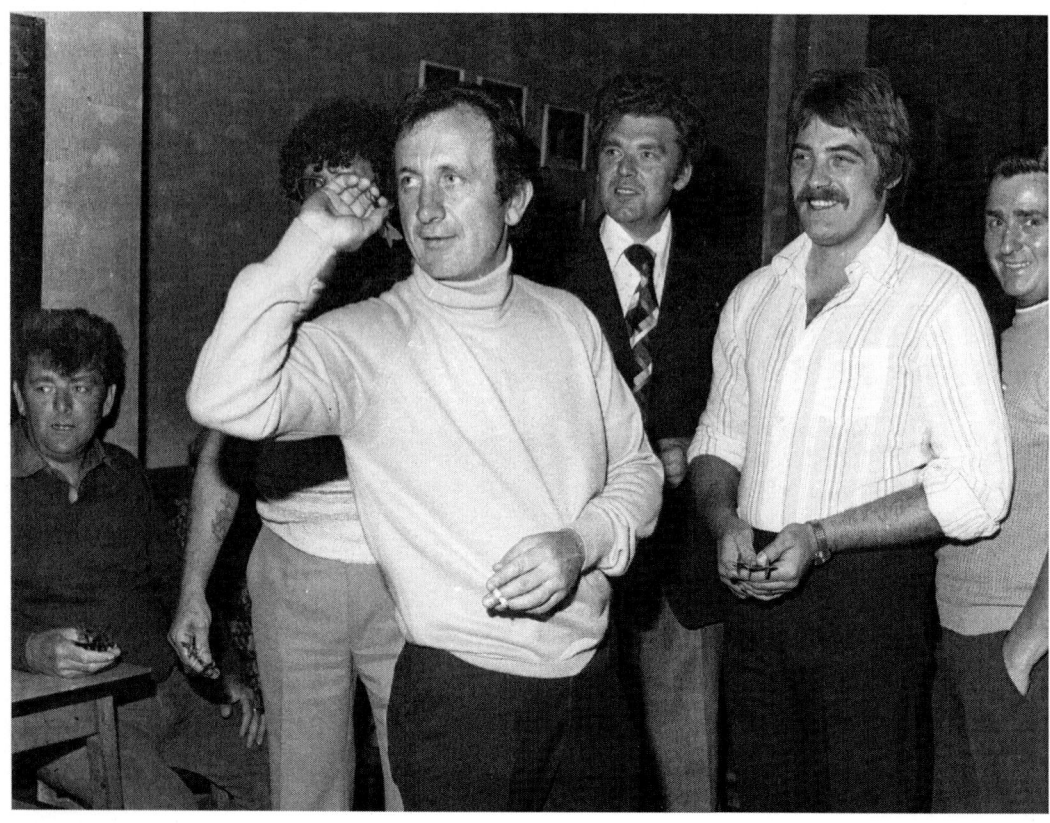

Above: The Alma Inn, Alfreton Road in 1972. The pub was built in 1936 replacing an older inn of the same name commemorating the famous battle of the Crimean war. Another Radford pub which has now closed.

Left: The Cricketers' Arms, Alfreton Road in 1972. From having a traditional name, the pub acquired the quirky title of Defatron's. Despite a new image, the pub has now closed.

The Windmill Inn, Alfreton Road in the mid-1960s, towards the end of its life. The pub, dwarfed by the new tower blocks of flats on Hartley Road, was shortly to be replaced by a new public house on the same site. The name evokes the windmills which once stood on the nearby Forest Road.

Opposite above: The Windmill, Alfreton Road in 1972. This functional pub was opened in 1966 to replace the earlier house of the same name – pictured above. After a spell as O'Grady's, the pub is now called the Local.

Opposite below: The Rose and Crown at the corner of Alfreton Road and Wood Street in 1972. The pub is now closed and awaiting conversion into shops and apartments.

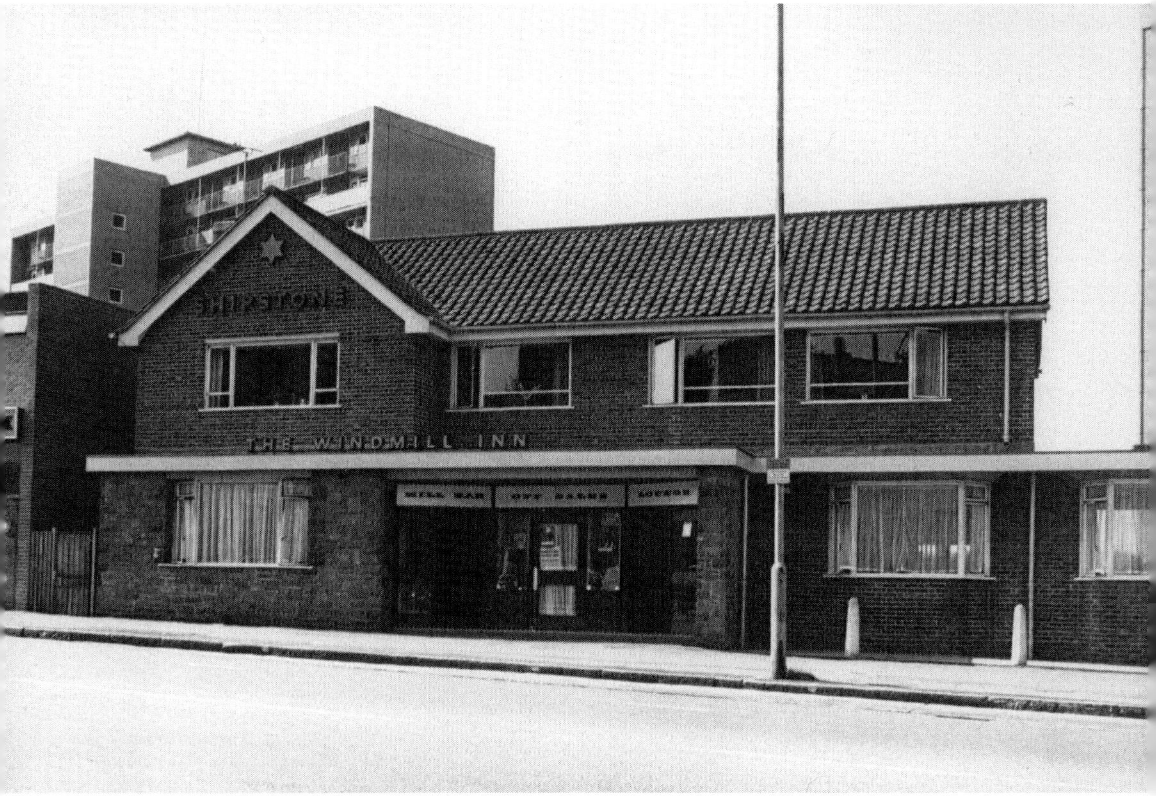
SHIPSTONE
THE WINDMILL INN

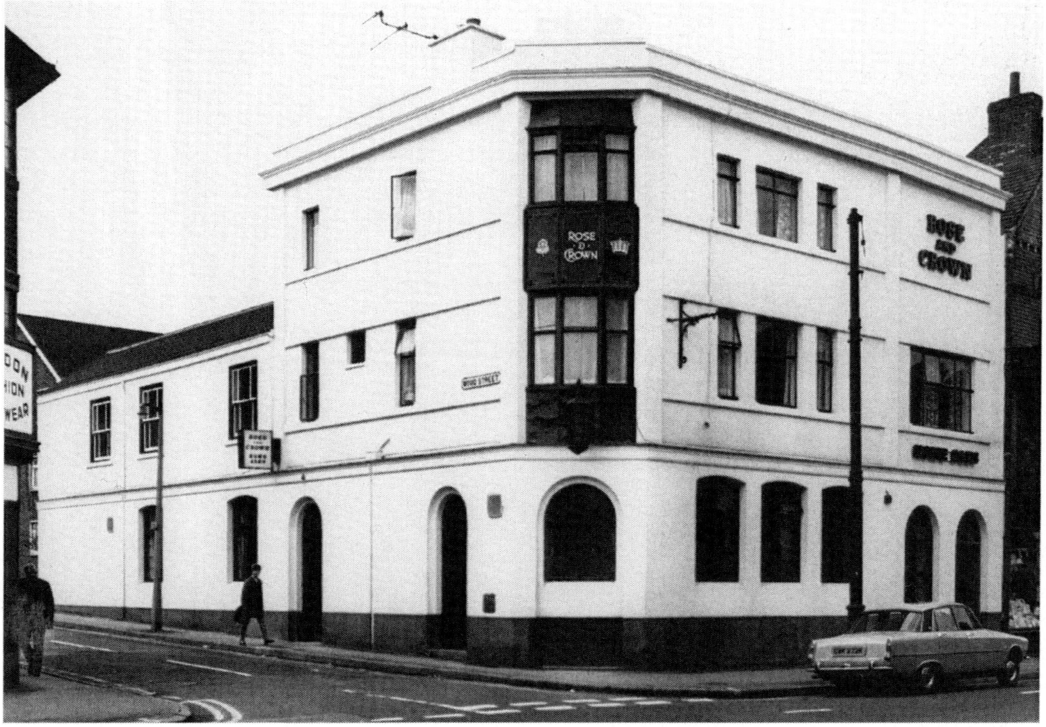
ROSE & CROWN

Left: The Running Horse, Alfreton Road in 1972, boasting a splendid green-tiled exterior. The pub which was well known for its musical evenings has now closed.

Below: The Falcon, Alfreton Road in 1972, with the now defunct Shipstone's sign on its exterior. The Falcon claims to have the best pub restaurant in the city.

Above: The Sir John Borlace Warren, Ilkeston Road in 1972. A commanding public house dating from 1814 and commemorating the locally born hero of the Battle of the Glorious First of June against the French in 1794. For some years, the exterior had the appearance of a Friesian cow, but new owners have removed the unsightly patches from the pub. The name sign has also been changed to the Sir John Borlase Warren, the correct spelling of the Admiral's name.

Left: The Dover Castle at the corner of Denman Street and Rifle Street in 1972. The pub, with its expansive windows, was formerly a working men's hotel. The Dover Castle has now been converted into flats.

A charabanc party outside the Jolly Higglers, Ilkeston Road in 1925. The ladies without exception all wearing hats, are due to set off on an excursion to Skegness. It was the convention at the time before leaving the neighbourhood pub to have a photograph taken of the group. The charabanc has a movable awning at the rear in the event of wet weather but the wheels are solid, which gives rather a hard ride.

The rebuilt and newly opened Jolly Higglers public house, Ilkeston Road in 1972. There are two explanations of the pub's title: a higgler being someone who bartered, or more probably in the case of this pub a worker who carried coal in a basket from an open-cast mine. The pub has now closed, with plans for it to be converted into a supermarket.

Above: The Sir Garnet Wolseley, Denman Street in 1972 when the licensee was Lancia Wright. The pub has lost its distinguished name and is now called the Globe. After closing, the building was converted into flats.

Left: The Marquis of Lorne, Salisbury Street, in 1972, when the landlord was Reginald Statham. A solidly built Victorian public house, like many other old pubs, the Marquis of Lorne has had a makeover, creating one large ground floor room.

OLD ROSE
INN
BARLEY WINE

TENNANTS
BARLEY WINE
TENNANTS
GREGORY HOTEL
GREGORY HOTEL

Piping in the new brew at the Gregory in 1977. Ida Allen, the wife of the landlord carrying tankards of beer into the bar, to the sound of the bagpipes. In the background is the host, Ernest Allen.

Opposite above: The Old Rose, St Peter's Street in 1972. The original pub, built in 1832, was named the Rose, a title it bore until 1900. The pub's Sunday evening raffles became very popular, generating money for pensioners' outings. The Old Rose has now closed down.

Opposite below: The Gregory, Ilkeston Road in 1972. The hotel was built in the 1880s at the same time as the boulevards were constructed through Lenton and Radford. This junction with Lenton Boulevard and Radford Boulevard was in the 1930s known as 'Ation Corner' from the buildings at each corner – damnation from the pub, ruination from the pawnbroker, education from the school and salvation from the church.

The Boulevard, Hartley Road in 1980. Another impressive Victorian hotel, built in 1883, with accommodation for the workers on the new roads then being built nearby. The hotel's advertisements of the period welcomed cyclists who were promised every comfort and first class food.

Opposite above: The Crown Hotel, Radford Marsh in 1934, shortly before its closure. The pub was scheduled for demolition in a road widening scheme with the licence being transferred to the new Crown built on a nearby site. In the distance is the Radford Railway Station and on the far left is the sign of the White Horse public house.

Opposite below: The Crown, at the junction of Wollaton Road and Western Boulevard in 1972 replacing the pub shown opposite above. When the Crown was built in 1935, this junction was relatively peaceful, but the nearby traffic island which now bears the pub's name, has a continuous stream of vehicles around it.

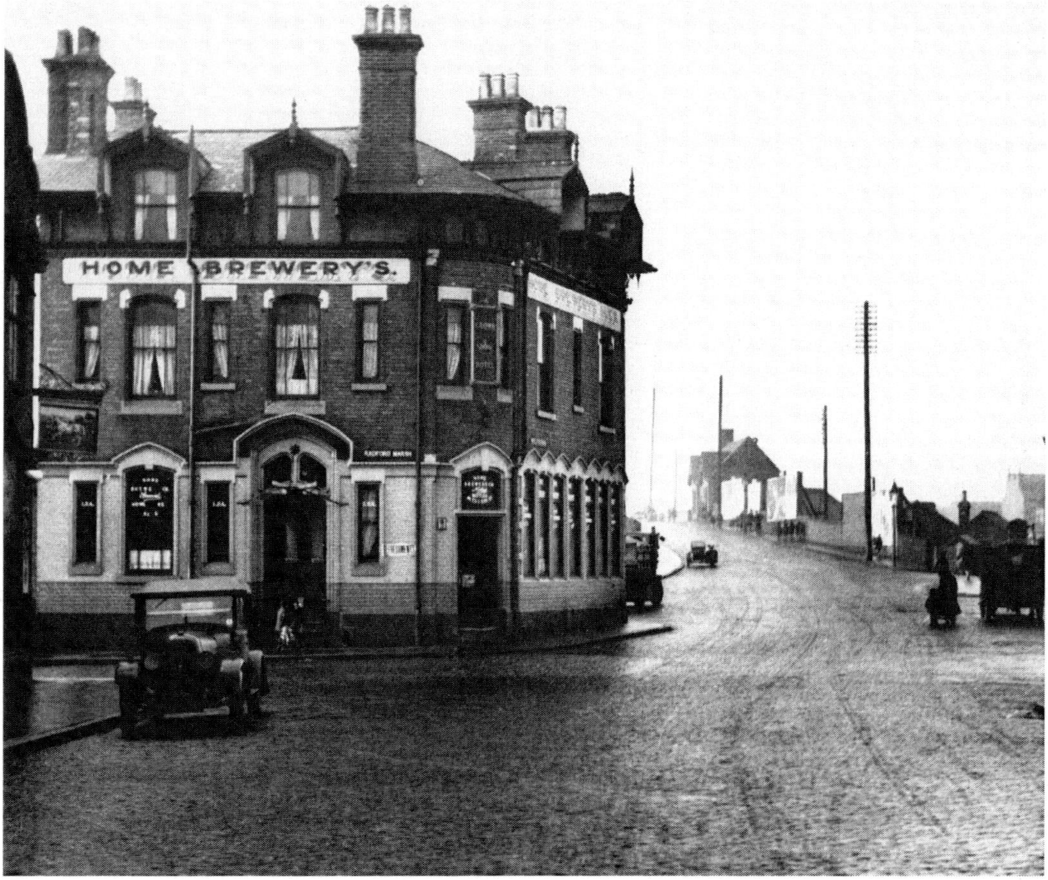
HOME BREWERY'S.

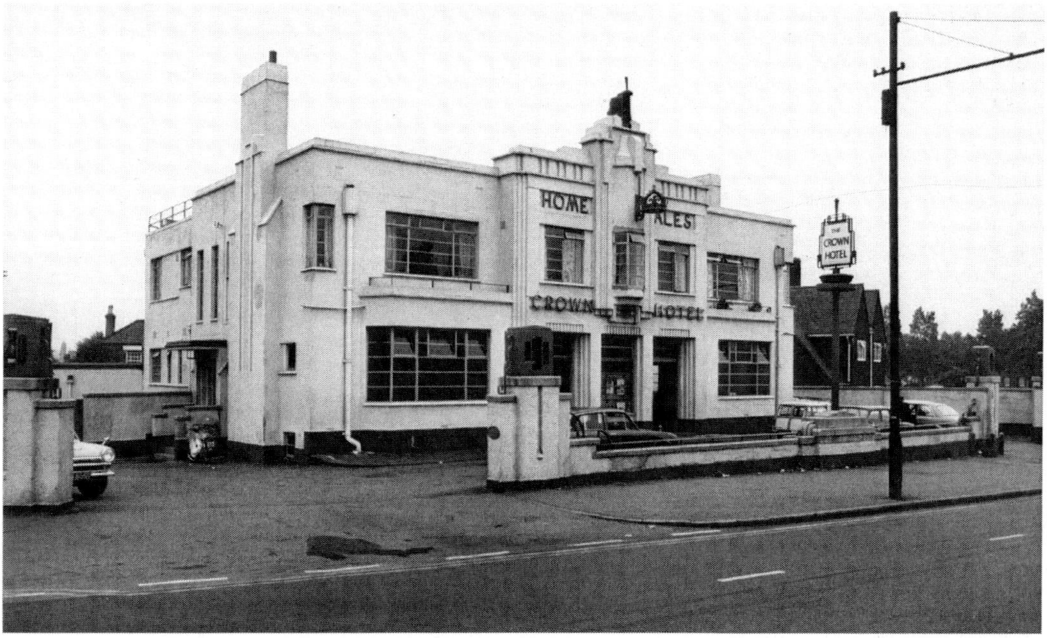
HOME ALES
CROWN HOTEL
CROWN HOTEL

The White Horse, Ilkeston Road in 1972. The pub was built in the Dutch style in 1912 on the site of an earlier coaching inn dating back to the sixteenth century. Its claim to fame is as the local pub of Arthur Seaton, the working-class hero of *Saturday Night and Sunday Morning*. In the opening episode of the Alan Sillitoe novel, after drinking eleven pints of beer and seven small gins, Seaton fell from the top to the bottom of the pub's stairs. This famous hostelry is now sadly closed.

Opposite above: The Three Wheatsheaves, Derby Road in the 1920s. Originally a farmhouse and later a beer house the Three Wheatsheaves was acquired by Shipstone's in 1938 from the Gregory family who had been lords of the manor since 1630.

Opposite below: The 17th/21st Lancers, Sherwin Street in 1972 was named after the old regiment of Colonel W.G. Hanson, then chairman of the Kimberley Brewery Company. Built on the site of the Albion, the pub was renamed the Dog and Topper, but has now closed to be replaced by a supermarket.

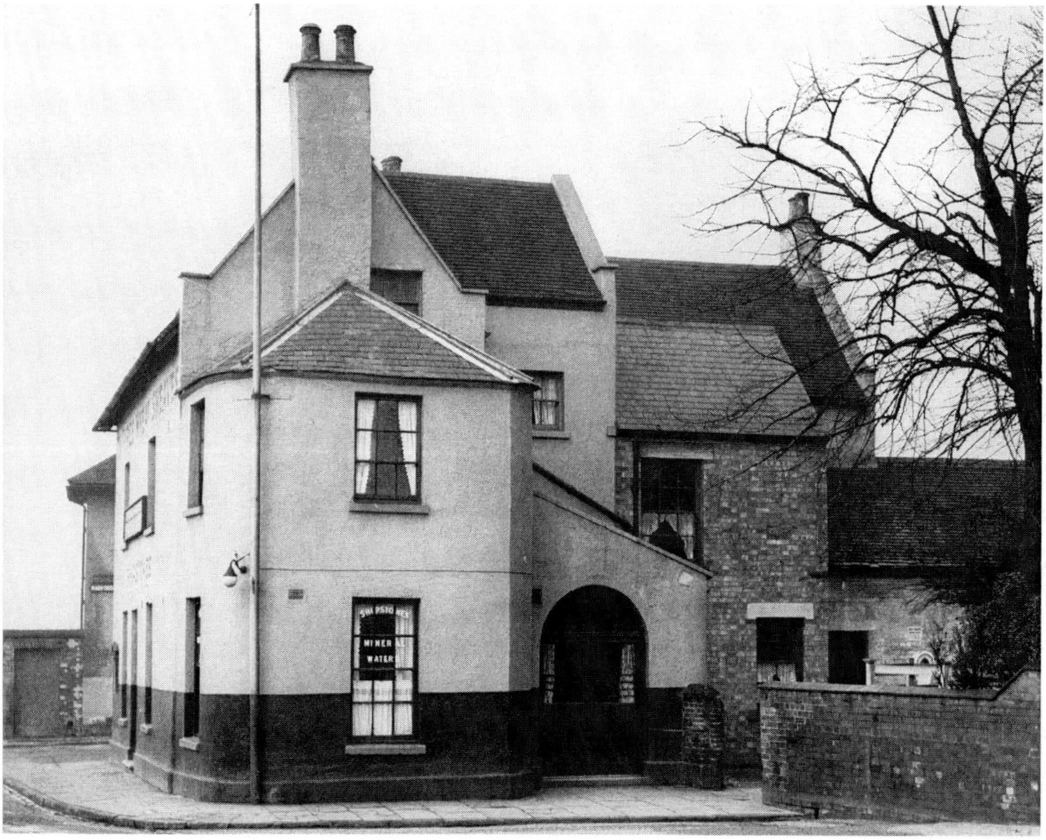
MINER
WATER

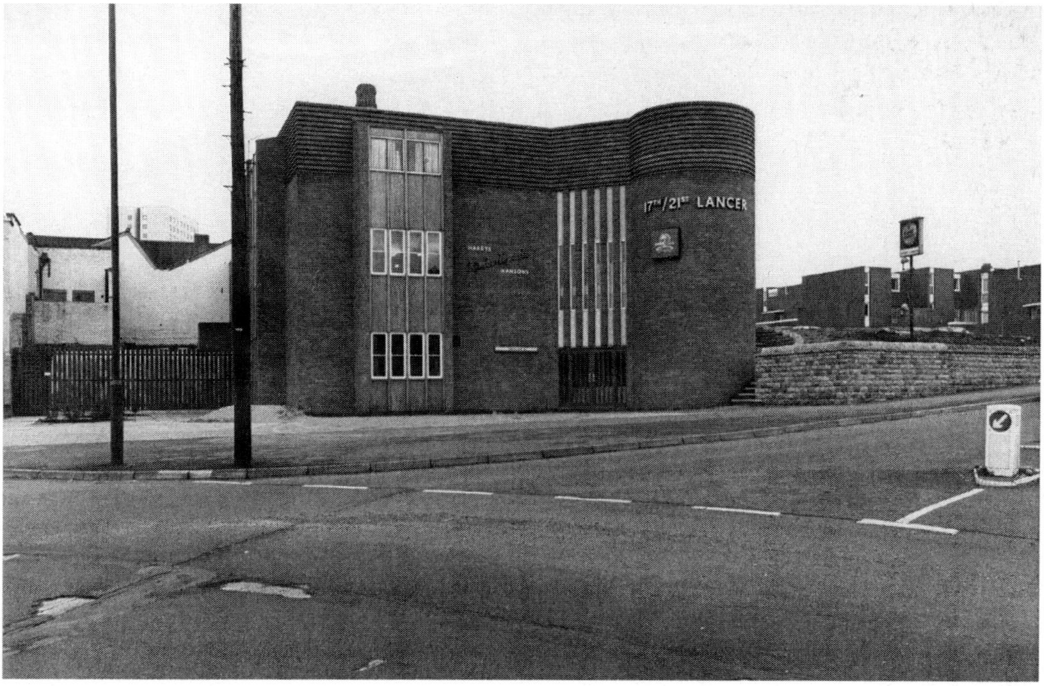
17th/21st LANCER

Left: The Boat Inn, Priory Street in 1972. The name is derived from the proximity of the River Leen and the Nottingham Canal. According to a local legend, a former landlord's deranged wife was burnt to death in an attic of the pub, despite her husband's desperate efforts to save her.

Below: The Johnson Arms, Abbey Street in 1972 was named after Frank Johnson, who rebuilt it in 1912. Originally known as the Abbey Tavern, it was frequented by the bargees on the nearby Nottingham Canal. The landlady when this photograph was taken was Grace Saunders.

The White Hart, Gregory Street in 1928. The inn was previously a farmhouse dating from the seventeenth century, which later became the Lenton Coffee House. In 1804, George Wombwell added a new frontage to the building and opened the White Hart which became the centre for all local activities. At the same time, one of the adjoining buildings became the Peverel prison for debtors, which remained here until 1842 when it was transferred to the Radford Workhouse in St Peter's Street. The White Hart has recently been refurbished but remains a welcoming pub with character.

If you are interested in purchasing other books published by The History Press, or in case you have difficulty finding any of our books in your local bookshop, you can also place orders directly through our website
www.thehistorypress.co.uk